PERSPECTIVES ON
AMERICAN PROGRESS

JACKIE ROBINSON BREAKS BARRIERS

BY DUCHESS HARRIS, JD, PHD
WITH TOM STREISSGUTH

Cover image: Jackie Robinson began playing for the Brooklyn Dodgers in 1947.

Core Library
An Imprint of Abdo Publishing
abdopublishing.com

abdopublishing.com

Published by Abdo Publishing, a division of ABDO, PO Box 398166, Minneapolis, Minnesota 55439.

Printed in the United States of America, North Mankato, Minnesota
032018
092018

THIS BOOK CONTAINS RECYCLED MATERIALS

Cover Photo: AP Images
Interior Photos: AP Images, 1, 10–11; Ray Howard/AP Images, 4–5, 43; TSN/Icon SMI/Newscom, 13; Jacob Harris/AP Images, 16–17; Bettmann/Getty Images, 20, 22–23, 36–37; Red Line Editorial, 25, 39; Sporting News Archive/Sporting News/Getty Images, 27; Harry Harris/AP Images, 30–31; Nina Leen/Time & Life Pictures/The LIFE Picture Collection/Getty Images, 32

Editor: Marie Pearson
Imprint Designer: Maggie Villaume
Series Design Direction: Ryan Gale

Library of Congress Control Number: 2017962652

Publisher's Cataloging-in-Publication Data

Names: Harris, Duchess, author. | Streissguth, Tom, author.
Title: Jackie Robinson breaks barriers / by Duchess Harris and Tom Streissguth.
Description: Minneapolis, Minnesota : Abdo Publishing, 2019. | Series: Perspectives on American progress | Includes online resources and index.
Identifiers: ISBN 9781532114922 (lib.bdg.) | ISBN 9781532154751 (ebook)
Subjects: LCSH: Robinson, Jackie, 1919-1972--Juvenile literature. | Major League Baseball (Organization)--Juvenile literature. | Race discrimination in sports--Juvenile literature. | Discrimination in sports--United States--History--Juvenile literature.
Classification: DDC 796.357092 [B]--dc23

CONTENTS

CHAPTER
ONE

NOT JUST A GAME

Opening day, 1947, brought 26,623 fans to Ebbets Field in New York City, New York. At the home of the Brooklyn Dodgers, the crowd watched history being made. In the seventh inning, the Dodgers trailed the Boston Braves by a run. The Dodgers' first hitter, Eddie Stanky, reached first base. That brought Jackie Robinson to home plate.

Robinson was the first African American to play major league baseball since Moses Fleetwood

Robinson stole 29 bases in his first season for the Dodgers.

Walker, a catcher for the 1884 Toledo Blue Stockings. So far he hadn't given the crowd much to cheer about. But if the Dodgers could get Stanky around all of the bases, they could tie the game. Robinson laid down a perfect bunt. Stanky scampered to second base while Boston's first baseman rushed his throw. The ball hit Robinson and sailed toward the outfield. Stanky and Robinson kept running, each gaining another base.

Up next, Pete Reiser hit a double, landing him on second base, and both Stanky and Robinson scored. The Dodgers took

WHAT'S A DODGER?

The Dodgers team dates to the 1850s. During that early era, baseball writers gave the teams often-changing nicknames. They named the Brooklyn squad the Atlantics, the Grays, the Bridegrooms, and then just the Grooms. In 1895, the writers came up with Trolley Dodgers. It was a grim fact that in the streets of Brooklyn new electric trolleys were running down many pedestrians. The name "Dodgers" first appeared on the team's uniform in 1933. That name stuck with the squad after it moved to Los Angeles, California, in 1958.

the lead and went on to win the game 5–3. Reiser got most of the attention in the next day's papers. But Jackie Robinson had proven that African Americans could succeed in baseball.

PERSPECTIVES

THE FIRST BLACK PLAYER

Moses Fleetwood Walker was the first African American to play in the big leagues. In 1884, the American Association admitted his Toledo, Ohio, Blue Stockings to the league. Walker didn't have the same athletic ability as Robinson. The Blue Stockings cut him at the end of the season. Walker's experiences made him feel as though black and white people would never get along. He wrote, "All experience, and every deduction from . . . human nature and human conduct are against the attempt to harmonize two alien races under the same government."

Taking a Chance

There was no rule against African Americans playing professional baseball. But many states kept the races apart by custom or by law. There seemed to be a silent agreement among team owners.

Only white men played major league baseball. For black men, the big leagues were out of bounds.

Branch Rickey, the Dodgers' general manager, signed Robinson to a contract in April 1947. Rickey knew he was taking a chance. There were owners, players, and fans who didn't want to see Robinson play in the big leagues. In their view, the sport should be segregated. Black players belonged in the separate leagues known as the Negro Leagues.

But Rickey believed in Jackie Robinson, and he wanted Robinson to play for the Dodgers. The team recruited him from the Kansas City Monarchs of the Negro Leagues. In 1946 Robinson played for Brooklyn's minor league team in Montreal, Canada. That year he led the International League with a .349 batting average. For Rickey, there was no reason to wait any longer. As one of the best players at the highest minor league level, Robinson was good enough for the Dodgers. This decision would change American sports forever.

STRAIGHT TO THE SOURCE

Judge Kenesaw Mountain Landis served as the commissioner of baseball for 24 years, from 1921 to 1944. Late in his career, he denied the game had a "color line." Speaking at a meeting in a New York hotel, he declared:

> *I want to make it clear that there is not, never has been, and as long as I am connected with baseball, there never will be any agreement among the teams or between any two teams, preventing Negroes from participating in organized baseball. Each manager is free to choose players regardless of race, color, or any other condition.*

Source: Marc Norton. "Jackie Robinson: I Never Had It Made." *Countercurrents.org*. Countercurrents.org, November 5, 2013. Web. Accessed October 12, 2017.

Back It Up

Judge Landis is using statements to make a point about segregation in baseball. Write a paragraph describing the point Landis is making. Then write down two or three pieces of evidence Landis uses to make the point.

CHAPTER
TWO

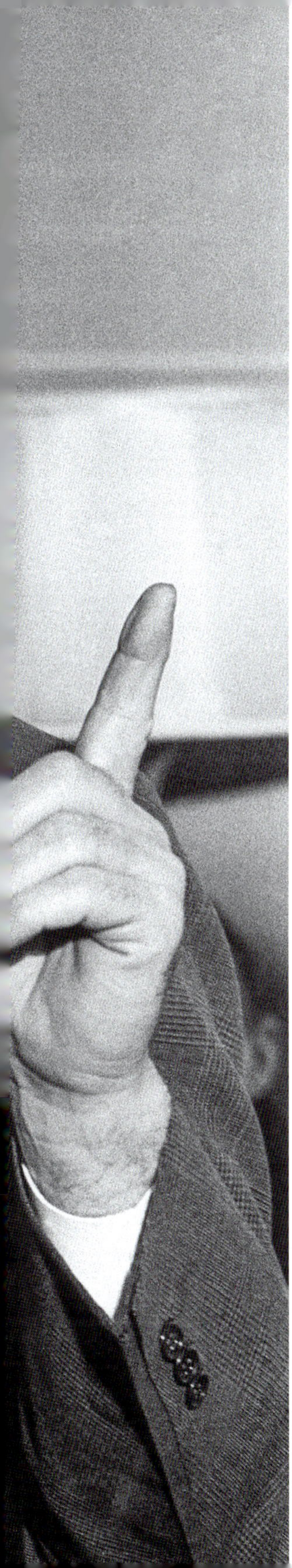

ON A CRUSADE

Branch Rickey was set on the integration of baseball. He wanted the Dodgers to be the first to bring African Americans to the major leagues. He knew there were good black players in the Negro Leagues. There was no reason they shouldn't have a chance to play for Brooklyn.

In 1945 Rickey sent his team of Dodger scouts out to games in the Negro Leagues. Their job was to search for good players. If anyone asked the reason, Rickey had a story ready. He claimed he wanted to form a new league of African-American pros. One of the teams, he said, would be the Brooklyn Brown Dodgers.

Branch Rickey became the Dodgers' general manager in 1942.

Jackie Robinson was one of Rickey's top prospects. At that time, Robinson played for the Kansas City Monarchs. He was a college graduate and a star athlete at the University of California, Los Angeles (UCLA). During World War II (1939–1945), he served in the US Army. He didn't smoke or drink, and he led a quiet personal life. Robinson had a temper, but Rickey believed that Robinson could turn this anger into good play on the baseball field.

Under Rickey's instructions, the Montreal Royals signed Robinson for the 1946 season. The Royals were one of the Dodgers' farm teams, from which the major league team could bring up good players.

THE INNOVATOR

Branch Rickey's most famous achievement was hiring Jackie Robinson. But he did much more for baseball. He also created the farm system, in which teams trained and prepared younger players on minor league teams. To protect the players, he encouraged the early use of batting helmets. The Dodgers were also one of the first teams to use batting cages and pitching machines.

Branch Rickey, *right*, helped the Dodgers make history by signing Robinson as the first black player.

That year, Robinson proved himself at the plate and on the field. He won the batting title for having the best batting average. He led the team to a championship.

Smart Business

The next spring, Rickey saw no reason to wait any longer. Other baseball clubs might be preparing to bring up a black player. Rickey called Robinson up to Brooklyn in April 1947. The Dodgers signed him to a rookie contract. Like all other big-league rookies, Robinson would earn the minimum salary: $5,000 for the season.

Rickey gave Robinson instructions on how he was to act. No matter what happened, the rookie must not answer taunts or insults. He should think only about the game. Rickey knew that any fighting or violence would set back integration in baseball. A controversy might slow or stop other black players from reaching the major leagues.

Robinson followed Rickey's instructions and kept his temper in check. He turned in a solid performance at first base, a position he had never played before. His .297 batting

PERSPECTIVES

THE PAPER TRAIL

Sports fans love to collect souvenirs. One of the most valuable is the original contract Jackie Robinson signed with the Brooklyn Dodgers. The contract was missing for many years. Finally, in 2013, a collector named Mykalai Kontilai came forward with a document he claimed to be the original. Kontilai also had a letter from Rachel Robinson, explaining that the document was authentic. An expert examined its ink and paper, and pronounced it real. The contract sold at auction in 2017 for $276,000.

average was good for a first-year player. That year, he was named the first Rookie of the Year in baseball history.

It was not an easy season. There was trouble with fans and other players. But Rickey's project succeeded. In 1948 he brought in Roy Campanella, a black catcher. Other teams began signing black players. Although laws still kept African Americans separate in many cities, the integration of baseball was underway.

FURTHER EVIDENCE

Chapter Two discusses Branch Rickey's efforts to bring Jackie Robinson to the big leagues. What is the main point of the chapter? Read the article on the website listed below. Does this article agree with that point? Does it give further evidence about Branch Rickey and why he wanted Jackie Robinson to play for the Dodgers?

NEWSDAY: JACKIE ROBINSON AND BRANCH RICKEY: TOGETHER IN HISTORY

abdocorelibrary.com/jackie-robinson

CHAPTER THREE

THE ACE AND THE ROOKIE

Ralph Branca began pitching for the Dodgers in 1944. He soon became the team's ace. Before the 1947 season began, Branca welcomed Robinson to the team. But many other Dodgers didn't want to play baseball with an African American. They sent around a petition demanding that the Dodgers get rid of Jackie Robinson or they would quit. Branca refused to sign it. On the day Robinson signed his big-league contract, Branca was there congratulating him.

Small gestures of friendship went a long way. When other Dodgers refused to speak to Robinson, Branca joined him on the field and

Ralph Branca, *left*, and Robinson became lifelong friends.

in the locker room. Branca often praised Robinson for good play on the field.

In one September 1947 game, the Dodgers were playing the Cardinals in Saint Louis, Missouri. A Cardinals player hit a foul ball high in the air. Robinson ran after it—and right toward the Brooklyn dugout. He got under the ball and made the catch. But his momentum was carrying him straight for the dugout steps. Branca rushed to break the fall. The collision carried both players to the ground. Branca had saved Robinson from a serious injury.

The tackle was a turning point in Robinson's career. His teammates seemed to relax. Robinson didn't hesitate to chase down dangerous fly balls, even when they were hit foul. He was working hard and taking risks. The Dodgers began to see him as a teammate.

That year, the Dodgers won the National League (NL) championship. By the time the World Series began in September, tensions between Robinson and his teammates eased. Winning made life easier on a baseball team.

A Bad Moment

Branca and Robinson remained teammates and friends. In 1951 the team was in an exciting race with the New York Giants. The teams were tied at the end of the season. They went to a three-game playoff to decide the NL championship.

In the final game, Branca had the worst moment of his career. He gave up a game-winning home run to the Giants' Bobby Thomson in the bottom of the ninth inning. As Thomson rounded the bases, Branca hung his

ALL-STARS

Branca was good enough to join the NL All-Star team in three different years. But Robinson outdid his teammate, appearing in six straight All-Star games from 1949 to 1954. In those days, fans voted for eight players who started the game on the field, and the All-Star teams' managers selected the rest of the rosters.

Dodgers
42

head in frustration. His Dodger teammates began trudging to the dugout. The home run won the championship for the Giants.

Robinson met up with Branca in the dugout. He was the only teammate to speak to him. By this time, Branca was crying in shame and anger. "Hang in there, Ralph," Robinson said. "If it wasn't for you, we wouldn't even be here."

PERSPECTIVES

THE LOVABLE LOSERS

Jackie Robinson was one of the best players on the Brooklyn Dodgers and in the NL. He helped the team win five NL pennants during his 10 years with the Dodgers. But the team had a lot of trouble in the World Series. They lost the championship to the New York Yankees in 1947, 1949, 1952, and 1953. Frustrated fans in Brooklyn would say, "Wait till next year!" Sportswriters liked to call Brooklyn's ballplayers the "lovable losers." But Robinson and the Dodgers finally beat the Yankees in the 1955 World Series.

Robinson, *bottom*, looks on as Branca, *right*, walks off the field after giving up the game to the Giants.

CHAPTER
FOUR

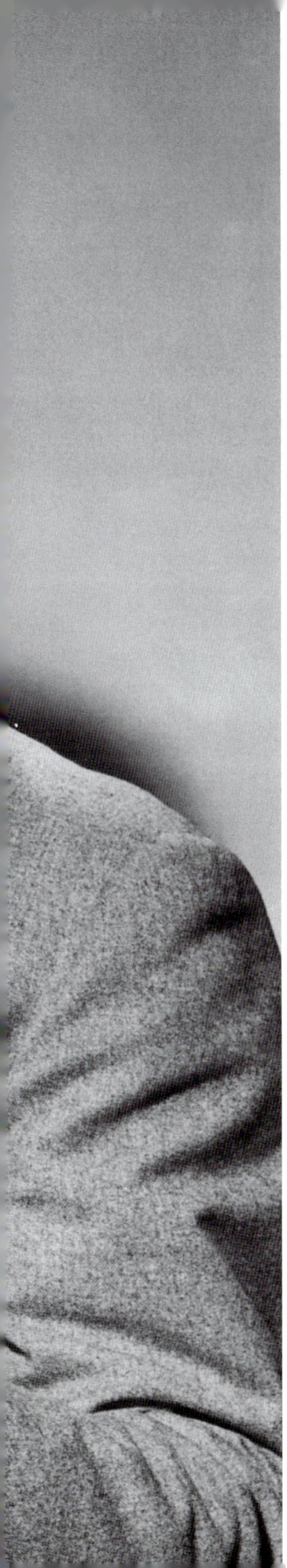

IN THE RADIO BOOTH

Red Barber was the Dodgers' radio broadcaster. In the era before television, radio was the only way for fans to follow a game live if they couldn't make it to the stadium. Barber was born in Columbus, Mississippi. His parents taught him to respect everyone he met. But in the South, there was a line not to be crossed. White people and black people did not socialize as equals. When Barber was growing up, black people were kept separate from white people on buses and in parks, schools, restaurants, and hotels.

Red Barber was a sports announcer for 33 years.

PERSPECTIVES

OUTSIDE THE STADIUM

As Robinson was integrating baseball, segregation still ruled in many parts of the country. Some states kept African Americans from voting. Black soldiers who risked their lives for the United States faced discrimination when they returned home. A law called the GI Bill was supposed to help veterans buy homes and get an education. But many banks and universities did not take applications from African Americans.

After Robinson retired from baseball, he kept battling for equality. "Life is not a spectator sport," he once said. "If you're going to spend your whole life in the grandstand just watching what goes on, in my opinion you're wasting your life."

The Secret

In 1945 Branch Rickey asked Barber to join him for a meal. The two men sat together in the back of a restaurant, with no one nearby to hear. Rickey revealed to Barber that he was bringing up a black player to play with the Dodgers. The Brown Dodgers were just a cover story. For the time being, the matter would remain a secret. Only a very few other people were in on it.

Barber left the restaurant surprised

THE TROPHY CASE

	1947	1948	1949	1950	1951	1952	1953	1954	1955	1956
Rookie of the Year	●									
Most Valuable Player			■							
All-Star Appearances			★	★	★	★	★	★		
Pennants	▲		▲			▲	▲		▲	▲
Championships									◆	

Jackie Robinson collected several honors and accomplishments during his major league career. His trophy cabinet includes NL Rookie of the Year and Most Valuable Player awards, a World Series title, and six appearances on the NL All-Star team. How do you think these accomplishments helped his teammates change from unfriendly to welcoming toward Robinson?

and confused. His first instinct was to quit his job. Despite his generally tolerant attitude, he could not see himself accepting a black player on the Dodgers. The Dodgers' general manager was upsetting the way things were done. Even as an announcer, he couldn't be associated with a mixed team. Another question occurred to him. Why did Rickey confide in him, a mere radio announcer, and so few others?

That evening, Barber's wife talked him out of quitting. She told him to think it over carefully before making a decision. If Rickey had decided to tell Barber, there must have been a reason. It might have something to do with the fact that Barber was the public voice of the Dodgers. And that voice had a southern accent.

Thinking It Over

Barber spent the 1946 season thinking hard about what Rickey had told him. He also thought about his own long-held beliefs and attitudes. Why could he not accept a black baseball player on the Dodgers' roster? Was it really his business whom the Dodgers chose to play? He had no say in running the team. His job was to simply describe the games over a radio microphone.

Barber thought back to something an umpire had once told him. Umpiring was just a matter of "umpiring the ball." Everything else in the game—the fans, the players, the managers, and the weather—really had

Besides announcing games over the radio, Barber also interviewed players.

Dodgers
NBC
1

no importance. The umpire's job was to call balls and strikes at home plate, shout "safe" or "out" in the infield, and keep a close eye on foul balls. At all times, he had to focus on the baseball. Of course, an announcer had to describe the players and the plays as well. But the ball was by far the most important thing on the field.

Barber didn't quit. He was in the Dodgers' radio booth on opening day in 1947 and remained there for many years. He came to realize that skin color wasn't important in baseball. It was a lesson he would never forget.

A NATIONAL TEAM

The 1947 Brooklyn Dodgers found themselves in a race for the league championship. Big crowds came to Ebbets Field for the games. By July 19, more than 1 million fans had come to the stadium to see a game that season—the best attendance record in the league. Robinson played a big role that year in spreading an interest in baseball across the country. Red Barber's radio broadcasts were heard across the nation. Audiences listened from Miami, Florida, to San Diego, California.

STRAIGHT TO THE SOURCE

General Colin Powell is an African American and son of Jamaican immigrants. Although a fan of the New York Giants, he was still rooting for Jackie Robinson in Brooklyn. In an interview, he remembered Robinson's first season.

> *Our approach was almost humorous, because that kind of humor was part of the culture. We said, "Oh Lord, don't let him strike out." The greatest fear was that he wouldn't do well, and that would be a mark against all of us. There were still no black Greyhound bus drivers, no black airline pilots. I still remember joking when Greyhound . . . hired its first black bus driver. "Oh Lord, just don't let him run into anything."*

Source: Jonathan Eig. *Opening Day: The Story of Jackie Robinson's First Season*. New York: Simon & Schuster, 2007. Print. 87.

What's the Big Idea?

Read this passage closely. What is the main idea Powell is stating? Write down two or three pieces of evidence he uses to support this point.

CHAPTER FIVE

HOME IN BROOKLYN

Rachel Isum grew up in Los Angeles. She met Jackie Robinson in 1941. They were both students at UCLA, where Rachel was studying to be a nurse. She graduated in 1945, and the couple married in early 1946.

This was at the start of Robinson's journey to the major leagues. That year, he played for the Montreal Royals. Rachel moved with him to Montreal. Their son Jack was born in the fall.

Rachel went to many of Robinson's home games.

Rachel postponed her own career to raise their children.

When the Dodgers called Robinson up the next spring, the family moved to New York City.

Big City

For Rachel, New York was a big change from sunny, warm California. The winters were cold, and the city streets seemed crowded and noisy. For a time, the family lived at the Hotel McAlpin in Manhattan. It was a good hotel, but not a home.

The season's opening day took place on April 15, 1947. Rachel left the hotel for the stadium. Holding the baby, she stood outside the hotel, trying to hail a cab. Several taxi drivers passed her by, even though the cabs had no passengers.

Finally, a taxi stopped to pick her up. She rode to the entrance of Ebbets Field. Rachel found her reserved seat and sat down with Jack. They were behind the Dodger dugout on the first-base side. She had a clear view of the field and the players. When someone sitting next to her offered to hold the baby, Rachel turned her full attention on her husband.

Moving to Brooklyn

Rachel went to many of the Dodgers' home games in Brooklyn, but wives were not allowed to travel with the team. This meant Robinson and Rachel spent a lot of time apart during Robinson's big-league career. The Robinsons eventually moved from the Hotel McAlpin to a house in Brooklyn. Robinson was gone a lot, so Rachel could not follow her dream of becoming a nurse. She had to care for their children.

Robinson's first year in the big leagues was hard. There was a lot of pressure on him to do well. At the same time, he had to live with the taunts of the fans

PERSPECTIVES

NEIGHBORS

When the Robinsons moved to young Steve Satlow's block in Brooklyn, Satlow was excited. He was a huge Dodgers fan. Late in 1948, the Robinsons found out their neighbors didn't have a Christmas tree. Robinson brought a tree to their front door. He didn't realize they didn't have a tree because they were Jewish. Still, they appreciated Robinson's gesture. The Satlows placed the tree next to their menorah, a candle holder used in Judaism. The two families decorated the tree that night. Rachel and Satlow's mother remained close friends for many years.

and other players. His home with Rachel was an escape from all the troubles. On the days he played well, they celebrated. They also talked about the many threats Robinson heard on the field.

At the end of Robinson's playing career, Rachel went to work. She also went back to school to earn a master's degree. The Yale University School of Nursing hired her as a professor. She suffered through the loss of her son in 1971, her husband in 1972, and her mother in 1973. In the years that followed, she started the Jackie Robinson Foundation. She kept up the fight for equal rights that they had been working toward since 1947.

CARRYING ON THE STORY

Rachel Robinson kept fighting for equal rights after her husband passed away. The Jackie Robinson Foundation (JRF) helps young people attend college by granting them scholarships. As a condition, JRF Scholars must take jobs serving the community while they're attending college.

EXPLORE ONLINE

Chapter Five discusses Rachel's experiences during Robinson's first game. The video at the website below also explores that first game. What information is the same? What additional information does it have?

MLB: RACHEL ROBINSON: JACKIE'S DEBUT

abdocorelibrary.com/jackie-robinson

CHAPTER SIX

BREAKING THE COLOR BARRIER

Jackie Robinson didn't like to back down. He had faced racism all his life, and he fought back. Sometimes this got him into trouble. One day, while serving in the US Army, he refused to move to the back of a bus. The army took him to court for insubordination. At the trial, he fought the charges. The judge cleared him.

But on opening day, 1947, Robinson would perform before thousands of fans. He remembered Branch Rickey's instructions. No matter what happened, he must control

Robinson was able to keep his head clear and play the game in spite of the racism he encountered.

his anger. And he did. In the seventh inning, he was a big part of the Dodgers' game-winning rally.

RETIRING NUMBER 42

Robinson wore number 42 during his first Dodgers game. The 50th anniversary of that game was April 15, 1997. On that day, Major League Baseball retired the number in Robinson's honor. No new player could use number 42. Players who already wore 42 were allowed to keep it. The last major leaguer to wear it retired after the 2013 season. Every major-league ballpark displays the retired numbers of the home team's greatest players. They also display number 42 in memory of Jackie Robinson.

Not Fighting Back

The first weeks of the 1947 season were rough. Robinson played well on the field. Like most rookies, he had a hard time adjusting to major league pitching. At this level, pitchers threw so much harder and more accurately than those in the minor leagues. The taunts and insults he heard from the stands didn't help.

BASEBALL INTEGRATION

Jackie Robinson was the first of many African-American big-league players in modern baseball. The percentage of African-American players grew through the 1980s. How do you think Robinson made it possible for so many more African-American players to join the big leagues?

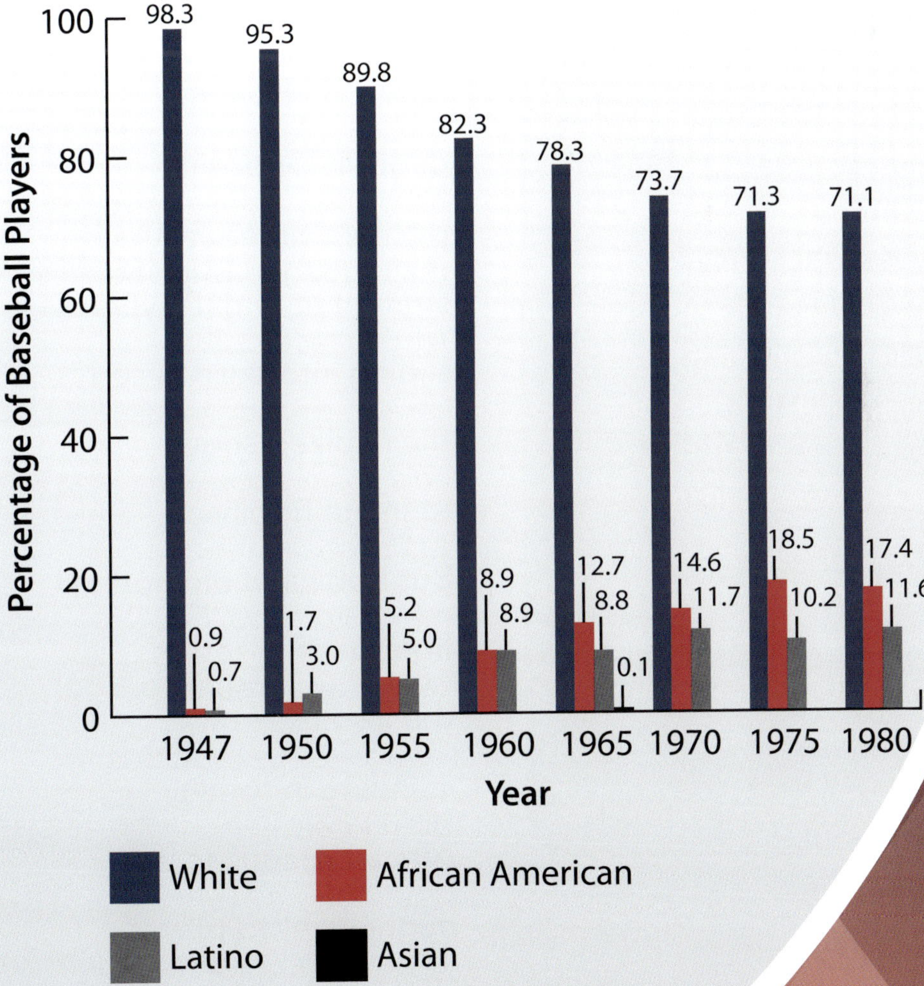

Opposing teams spewed bad words at him. Philadelphia Phillies manager Ben Chapman used every racist word he could think of to harass Robinson from the dugout. Opposing pitchers aimed fastballs straight at him. Players sliding into base raised their spiked shoes to injure Robinson. But Robinson did not fight back or return the insults. He was standing in for any African American who might want to play

PERSPECTIVES

MAKING MANAGER

Jackie Robinson wanted to manage a big-league team. But by the time of his death on October 24, 1972, there were still no big-league black managers. Things changed on May 8, 1973. After an argument, an umpire threw Chicago Cubs manager Whitey Lockman out of the game. Lockman handed Ernie Banks the lineup card. For the first time in history, an African American was managing a major league baseball team. The Cubs won the game. "Nobody said anything to me," Banks later said. "Not a writer, nobody called me, none of that."

big-league baseball. Fighting or even playing poorly would set them all back. He needed to play well and ignore everything but the game.

A Good Year

Robinson had a good first year with the Dodgers. He played strong defense at first base and proved himself a smart base runner. He had slumps and hitting streaks. But by the end of the season, opponents grew to respect him as much as any other good player.

Most fans grew used to a black man playing professional baseball. With his solid play, Robinson proved there should be no color barrier in baseball. A skilled and smart athlete could help a team win no matter their skin color. That year, Robinson helped the Dodgers win the pennant and go to the World Series. They lost the Series. But Jackie Robinson had beat baseball's color line.

IMPORTANT DATES

1945
Branch Rickey scouts for good players in the Negro Leagues. He tells Red Barber of his plan to sign a black player with the Dodgers.

1946
Jackie Robinson marries Rachel Isum. Robinson plays for the Montreal Royals.

1947
Robinson signs a contract to play with the Dodgers in April. He helps the Dodgers win the opening game on April 15. One million fans come to Ebbets Field on July 19.

1948
Roy Campanella, a black catcher, joins the Dodgers.

1955
Robinson and the Dodgers win the World Series.

1972
Robinson dies on October 24.

1973
Ernie Banks becomes the first African American to manage a major league baseball team on May 8.

1997
Major League Baseball retires Robinson's number on April 15.

STOP AND THINK

Dig Deeper

After reading this book, what questions do you still have about Jackie or Rachel Robinson? With an adult's help, find a few reliable sources that can help you answer your questions. Write a paragraph about what you learned.

Take a Stand

Branch Rickey told Jackie Robinson to not fight back when other players insulted him. Do you think that it was smart for Robinson to not respond when people said mean things to him? Or do you think he should have fought back? Why?

Why Do I Care?

Maybe you do not play baseball. But that doesn't mean you can't think about ways Jackie Robinson made life better for people in the United States. How did breaking the color barrier affect who plays professional sports today? What are some issues that Robinson faced in his career that you still see today?

GLOSSARY

ace
a baseball team's best pitcher

batting average
a ratio that tells how many times a batter reached base on a hit (single, double, triple, or home run) for every time at bat

bunt
to bump the baseball with the bat instead of swinging

dugout
in baseball, the low, sheltered bench area where each team sits during a game

infield
the part of a baseball field from home plate to the edge of the outfield grass

inning
the division of a baseball game where each team gets a chance to bat and that ends at their third out

insubordination
the act of not obeying an authority

outfield
the part of a baseball field from the edge of the infield to the home run fence

pennant
a flag that symbolizes a team winning a league championship

segregated
separated because of traits such as race

ONLINE RESOURCES

To learn more about Jackie Robinson, visit our free resource websites below.

Core Library
CONNECTION
FREE! COMMON CORE MULTIMEDIA RESOURCES

Visit **abdocorelibrary.com** for free Common Core resources for teachers and students, including vetted activities, multimedia, and booklinks, for deeper subject comprehension.

Booklinks
NONFICTION NETWORK
FREE! ONLINE NONFICTION RESOURCES

Visit **abdobooklinks.com** for free additional online weblinks for further learning. These links are routinely monitored and updated to provide the most current information available.

LEARN MORE

Herman, Gail. *Who Was Jackie Robinson?* New York: Grosset & Dunlap, 2011.

Smolka, Bo. *Jackie Robinson Breaks the Color Barrier.* Minneapolis, MN: Abdo, 2015.

ABOUT THE AUTHORS

Duchess Harris, JD, PhD

Professor Harris is the chair of the American Studies department at Macalester College and curator of the Duchess Harris Collection of ABDO books. She is the author and coauthor of recently released ABDO books including *Hidden Human Computers: The Black Women of NASA*, *Black Lives Matter*, and *Race and Policing*.

Before working with ABDO, she authored several other books on the topics of race, culture, and American history. She served as an associate editor for *Litigation News*, the American Bar Association Section of Litigation's quarterly flagship publication, and was the first editor in chief of *Law Raza*, an interactive online journal covering race and the law, published at William Mitchell College of Law. She has earned a PhD in American Studies from the University of Minnesota and a JD from William Mitchell College of Law.

Tom Streissguth

The author of more than 100 nonfiction books for young readers, Tom Streissguth has worked as an editor, journalist, and teacher and has traveled widely in Asia, Europe, and the Middle East. He lives in Minnesota, where he works on books and enjoys part-time jobs that keep him active in the great outdoors.

INDEX